Breaking the Cycle

Moving past the curse!

Darlene Greene

Copyright © 2015 Darlene Greene. All rights reserved. No portion of this book may be reproduced mechanically, electronically, or by any other means, including photocopying, without written permission of the publisher. It is illegal to copy this book, post it to a website, or distribute it by any other means without permission from the publisher.

Darlene Greene
Street Address: 4416 S. Carrier Pky #280
City, State and ZIP Code: 75052
Phone Number 972-290-0742
Email Address dargreene@inamaegreene.org
Website Address www.inamaegreene.org

Limits of Liability and Disclaimer of Warranty

The author and publisher shall not be liable for your misuse of this material. This book is strictly for informational and educational purposes.

Warning – Disclaimer

The purpose of this book is to educate and entertain. The author and/or publisher do not guarantee that anyone following these techniques, suggestions, tips, ideas, or strategies will become successful. The author and/or publisher shall have neither liability nor responsibility to anyone with respect to any loss or damage caused, or alleged to be caused, directly or indirectly by the information contained in this book

DOMESTIC ABUSE IS A CYCLE NOT A CURSE!

No one deserves to be abused. This is victim-blaming mentality, which focuses on the survivor's behavior instead of the perpetrators. Whether it's coming home late, wearing something "unapproved" or forgetting to put gas in the car, abuse is never warranted. Making you feel like you deserved the abuse is a way for an abusive partner to avoid accountability by shifting the blame to you. Other ways of not taking responsibility: blaming the relationship, childhood, health problems, substance abuse, children, etc. But you don't need to be a victim! You can take back your life and live free of abuse.

We know that leaving is not only difficult but it can also be dangerous. But if you have reached that point in your self awareness, and you are ready to leave; and you are reading this book; likely you have connected with a shelter or victim service agency like The Ina Mae Greene Foundation-For My Sisters that is helping you find the resources you need to get out of your abusive relationship situation.

This book is going to be a source of strength and inspiration for you. It is filled with my favorite prayers and quotes that I still use when I am feeling overwhelmed or discouraged. I am confident that they will help you also. Help you to remember that you deserve to be safe and you deserve a life without fear and pain. So on the days you are feeling low, or feeling that you are not going to make it through the struggle, turn to the page that is going to get you through that temporary fear of change. The quote, prayer or saying, that will help get you past the fear of moving forward and taking back your life. Sometime life changes, although necessary, can be difficult; but remember you not alone. We who have lived through this crime have all felt that same fear. The same fear of change we all had before we left the life of abuse behind. It is going to be scary sometimes, but you can do it!

Get your felt tip color markers and mark away. Underline, outline and circle the pages, the phases and the chapters that bring you back to the place you need to be, a place of putting your health and safety first!

CONTENTS

Introduction

Dreams

Courage

Failure

Perspective

Excuses

Faith

Hope

DREAMS

Without them the future tastes bland.

I am able to do all things through Him who strengthens me.

~ Philippians 4:13

"The greatest achievements were at first and for a time dreams. The oak sleeps in the acorn."

~James Allen

All of humanity's amazing accomplishments were once the seeds of someone's dreams.

To get through difficult times in your life you need to remember the dreams you had for your life before the abuse started, before you met HIM. What did you see yourself discovering, learning, traveling too, creating etc.

Remember that dream, it is not to late, you are starting your life over, go back and pick up that dream, and make it a reality!

~Darlene Greene

"Dreams are today's answers to tomorrow's questions."

~Edgar Cayce

"Hold fast to dreams, for if dreams die, life is a broken-winged bird that cannot fly."

~*Langston Hughes*

If we give up on our dreams we give up that which differentiates us from all other creatures—and life becomes condensed to only survival.

"There is only one thing that makes a dream impossible to achieve; the fear of failure."

~Paulo Coelho

Most of what stands in the way of our dreams is us. Dare to get out of your own way.

"Dare to live the life you have dreamed for yourself. Go forward and make your dreams come true."

~Ralph Waldo Emerson

You are the engine that fuels your dreams into reality—your participation is paramount.

"If you can dream it, you can do it. Always remember that this whole thing was started with a dream and a mouse."

~Walt Disney

Your mouse is better than Walt's mouse! His didn't even have the Internet.

"A dream plus a deadline equals a goal achieved."

~Donna Kozik

If you want your dreams to come true—you have to create a space for them to exist. When you give yourself a deadline you invite your dreams into the real world.

Don't give up on your dreams they are the blueprints for your future!

~Darlene Greene

"Whatever you can do, or dream you can, begin it. Boldness has genius, power and magic in it."

~Johann Van Goeth

Your actions propel your dreams into reality.

COURAGE

It's not for the faint of heart.

But he said to them, "Why are you fearful, you of little faith?" Then he got up and rebuked the winds and the sea. And there was a great calm.
~*Matthew 8:26*

"It is not because things are difficult that we do not dare; it is because we do not dare that things are difficult."

~Seneca

Courage expressed has a way of changing obstacles into hurdles.

"There is the risk you cannot afford to take, and there is the risk you cannot afford not to take."

~Peter Drucker

Isn't it better to regret the things you *did* than the things you *didn't?*

"Trust that still, small voice that says, "This might work and I'll try it."

~*Diane Mariechild*

Make friends with that voice. It knows things.

"Courage is not the absence of fear, but rather the judgment that something else is more important than fear."

~Ambrose Redmoon

When your fear of failure is less important than your need to try, courage has a place to breathe.

"Courage doesn't always roar. Sometimes courage is the quiet voice at the end of the day saying, "I will try again tomorrow."

~Mary Anne Radmacher

Spend a few minutes watching a toddler who is learning to walk—that's courage in motion.

"Fear and courage are brothers."

~*Proverb*

While fear knows nothing of courage, courage knows fear intimately.

"If you have the courage to begin, you have the courage to succeed."

~David Viscott

You don't fall up a mountain. You reach the summit by taking one step after another.

Your courage has gotten you this far, don't stop now. Dig deep, you have the courage that will allow you to take the steps that will lead you to the finish-to taking back your life; so keep moving. Although it may be hard at times, and you may feel that you can't go on, you can!

Keep moving forward, YOU ARE WORTH IT!

~Darlene Greene

"Life shrinks or expands in proportion to one's courage."

~*Anais Nin*

Got courage?

FAILURE

The mother of success.

One thing I do, forgetting those things, which are behind, and reaching forward to those things which are ahead, I press toward the goal for the prize of the upward call of God in Christ Jesus.

~Philippians 3:13-14

"I have not failed. I've just found 10,000 ways that won't work."

~Thomas Edison

Your perception of the efforts you make on the road to success makes a big difference in the ultimate outcome.

"Fall down seven times. Stand up eight."

~*Chinese Proverb*

Tap into your inner toddler.

"Failure is an event, never a person."

~William D. Brown

Unsuccessful attempts do not define who you are. Henry Ford failed at his first five business attempts.

"The men who try to do something and fail are infinitely better than those who try to do nothing and succeed."

~*Lloyd Jones*

The only way to really avoid the possibility of failure—do nothing—also ensures you won't have to deal with success.

"Never confuse a single defeat with a final defeat."

~F. Scott Fitzgerald

Embrace your failures. There is much to learn from them about what doesn't work.

Failure? Not an option when you are taking back your life. Move like your life depends on it, because it does!

~Darlene Greene

"Failure is the condiment that gives success its flavor."

~*Truman Capote*

If success was the only possible outcome, what would motivate us to be anything but complacent?

"Only those who dare to fail greatly can ever achieve greatly."

> ~*Robert F. Kennedy*

If you wanna be a trapeze artist, you gotta risk falling on your face.

"If we will be quiet and ready enough, we shall find compensation in every disappointment."

~Henry David Thoreau

There is often much more to be learned from our failed attempts at anything than there is from our successes.

PERSPECTIVE

Use it or lose it.

Therefore don't worry about tomorrow, because tomorrow will worry about itself. Each day has enough trouble of its own.

~Matthew 6:34

"There is no burnt rice to a hungry person."

~Philippine Proverb

Your powers of perception are the most important tools you have to navigate your way through life. Use them wisely.

"We can complain because rose bushes have thorns, or rejoice because thorn bushes have roses."

~Abraham Lincoln

How you see the world directly impacts how the world sees you. If you don't like how you are perceived, change the way you look at things.

"It is a narrow mind which cannot look at subjects from various points of view."

~George Elliot

When you take the time to look at things from many angles you not only expand your awareness, you multiply your opportunities.

"Everything can be taken from a man but one thing: the last of the human freedoms—to choose one's attitude in any given set of circumstances, to choose one's own way."

~Viktor E. Frankl

Attitude and perspective are intertwined. Whether you are mindful of your perspective or not, your attitude will reflect it.

"What we see mainly depends on what we look for."

~John Lubbuck

Challenge yourself to see something or someone differently and watch what happens.

"What you see and hear depends a good deal on where you are standing; it also depends on what sort of person you are."

~C.S. Lewis

No amount of prodding can make a grumpy person congenial. Only they can decide how they see the world.

"Loving people live in a loving world. Hostile people live in a hostile world. Same world."

~Wayne Dyer

Every parent knows a teenager looking for trouble will surely find it. What are you looking for?

Set real and attainable goals. You didn't get in this situation overnight and it is going to take some time to get use to a new way of thinking and living. Keep things in perspective, there are going to be setbacks, don't look at them as a failure, look at them as an opportunity to do it over, only better this time because now you know what will not work!

~Darlene Greene

"Life is ten percent what you make it and ninety percent how you take it."

~*Irving Berlin*

It's not really about what shows up in your world as much as it is what you decide to do about it.

"And those who were seen dancing, were thought to be crazy, by those who could not hear the music."

~Friedrich Nietzsche

Your perception of what someone else may be trying to accomplish may not accurately reflect his or her reality.

EXCUSES

They're rather unbecoming.

Consider it a great joy, my brothers, whenever you experience various trials, knowing that the testing of your faith produces endurance. But endurance must do its complete work, so that you may be mature and complete lacking nothing.

~James 1:2-4

"The person who really wants to do something finds a way; the other person finds an excuse."

~Author Unknown

No one really believes the dogs ate the homework anyway—why bother with such silliness?

"Never ruin an apology with an excuse."
~Kimberly Johnson

Sometimes it is better to be excused than to excuse oneself.

"It is better to offer no excuse than a bad one."

~George Washington

If there is no excuse for what you have or haven't done there's no point in compounding the situation.

"It is wise to direct your anger towards problems—not people, to focus your energies on answers—not excuses."

~William Arthur Ward

Every minute spent constructing or elaborating an excuse costs you sixty seconds of solution finding.

"I attribute my success to this: I never gave or took an excuse."

~Florence Nightingale

Never offer an excuse you wouldn't accept.

"If you don't want to do something, one excuse is as good as another."

~Yiddish Proverb

Why waste time making excuses for what you don't want to do instead of making progress with what you do want to do?

"Excuses are the tools with which persons with no purpose in view build for themselves great monuments of nothing."

~*Stephen Grayhm*

No one makes excuses for getting things done.

"No one ever excused his way to success."

~Dave Del Dotto

You cannot attain excellence in anything by making excuses for mediocre results.

As you know, we count as blessed those who have persevered. You have heard of Job's endurance and have seen the outcome from the Lord: the Lord is very compassionate and merciful.

~James 5:11

FAITH

The energy we need to do the impossible!

I assure you: If anyone says to the mountain, "Be lifted up and thrown into the sea," and does not doubt in his heart, but believes that what he says will happen, it will be done for him.

~Mark 11:23

Before you start the race have faith that you will finish it.

You have gone this far, don't give up now, your dreams, your courage, your faith, and hope for a better life have gotten you this far, and can take you the rest of the way. Remember you deserve to live; you deserve a life without fear, and pain.

Being safe at home is a right not a privilege, keep moving. If you need to stop long enough to cry, or take a breath, go ahead and cry. Take a deep breath but keep going, don't give up, you are almost at the finish!

~Darlene Greene

Faith is taking the first step even when you don't see the whole staircase.

~*Martina Luther King Jr.*

Watch, stand fast in the faith, be brave, be strong
~ *I Corinthians*

There are going to be times during this transition that everyone in your life, that you look to for support, and help, to get you through this trial, are going to be unavailable to help you, or encourage you one day. That is a time when you are going to need to tap into your faith. Your faith in God and your faith in your own ability to get yourself out of this situation.

Your friends and family might be busy on that day when you really need to be encouraged. But you cannot give up, and stop fighting. Because they are busy one day, does not mean that they don't love you, and want to help you, but simply they are involved in their own life and challenges, on that day when you need them so much. But do not be discouraged; they will be there for you again, keep moving forward and, KEEP THE FAITH!

~Darlene Greene

Be faithful in small things because it is in them that your strength lies.

~Mother Teresa

We are twice armed if we fight with faith.

~Plato

And the prayer offered in faith will make the sick person well; the Lord will raise them up.

~James 5:15

In faith there is enough light for those who want to believe and enough shadows to blind those who don't

~Blaise Pascal

Start by doing what's necessary; then do what's possible; and suddenly you are doing the impossible.

~Francis of Assisi

Life is not a problem to be solved, but a reality to be experienced.

~Soren Kierkegaard

HOPE

Hope always belongs to you, no one can take it away unless you let them.

Once you choose hope, anything's possible.
~*Christopher Reeve*

Hope is some extraordinary spiritual grace that God gives us to control our fears, not to oust them.

~Vincent McNabb

When the world says, "Give up," Hope whispers, "Try it one more time."

~Author Unknown

The wings of hope carry us, soaring high above the driving winds of life.

~Ana Jacob

All it takes is one bloom of hope to make a spiritual garden.

~Terri Guillemets

Hope is faith holding out its hand in the dark.

~*George Iles*

Hope is putting faith to work when doubting would be easier.

~*Author Unknown*

Never deprive someone of hope — it may be all they have.

Hope never abandons you, you abandon it.

~*George Weinberg*

Some see a hopeless end, while others see an endless hope.

Hope is the only bee that makes honey without flowers.

~*Robert Ingersoll*

"Hope is the thing with feathers
That perches in the soul
And sings the tune without the words
And never stops at all."
~*Emily Dickerson*

"Life's under no obligation to give us what we expect."
~*Margret Mitchell*

You may say I'm a dreamer, but I'm not the only one. I hope someday you'll join us. And the world will live as one."

~*John Lennon*

"And now these three remain: faith, hope and love. But the greatest of these is love."

~*Holy Bible King James version-Anonymous*

Martin Luther King, Jr.

We must accept finite disappointment, but we must never lose infinite hope.

John F. Kennedy

We should not let our fears hold us back from pursuing our hopes.

Scottish Proverb

Were it not for hope the heart would break.

Francois De La Rochefoucauld

We promise according to our hopes and perform according to our fears.

Mother Teresa

To keep a lamp burning, we have to keep putting oil in it.

But if we hope for what we do not see, we eagerly wait for it with patience.

~Romans 8:25

Hope is being able to see that there is light despite all of the darkness.

Desmond Tutu

A word spoken at the right time is like golden apples on a silver tray

~Proverbs 25:11

When you embrace hope you are giving yourself a fighting chance. So never let go of hope, even if everything looks as if it is not going to go as planned, don't give up hope.

It is your light in the storm. And never allow anyone to dash your hope, it is for you and you alone, take special care. It is precious!

~Darlene Greene

Conclusion

Remember to DREAM, they feed your HOPE and give you the COURAGE to find your own peace. Keep your goals in PERSPECTIVE and don't fear FAILURE because that is only an EXCUSE to quit. Keep the FAITH and never ever give up HOPE!

Give Me Strength Lord

"Lord, you are Holy above all others, and all of the strength that I need is in your hands. Lord I am not asking that you take this trial away, instead, I simply ask that your will be done in my life. But I admit that it's hard sometimes Lord. Sometimes I feel like I can't go on. Often the pain and the fear are too much for me and I know that I don't have the strength on my own to get through this trial. I know that I can come to you Jesus and that you will hear my prayer. I know that it is not your intent to bring me to this point just to leave me in the wilderness alone.

Please Lord, give me the strength that I need to face today; I don't have to worry about tomorrow. If you just give me the strength that I need to face today that is all I need. Keep me from sinning during this trial. Instead help me to keep my eyes on you. You are the Holy Lord and all of my hope rest in you."

In Jesus name Amen

NOTES

MY OWN THOUGHTS

SAFETY PLAN WORKBOOK

Personal Safety Plan Workbook

Often if you write something out it is easier to remember, this workbook will assist you in thinking through some issues that will be important if you are planning to leave your abuser.

Step 1: Safety during a violent incident

Women cannot always avoid violent incidents. In order to increase safety, battered women may use a variety of strategies. This is just a few of the things that you might think about to help you stay safe in a violent situation: Your shelter will be happy to help you with your safety plan if you are not sure how to begin.

A. If I decide to leave, I will

_____

_____

_____

_____

(Practice how to get out safely. What doors, windows, elevators, stairwells or fire escapes will you use?)

B. I can keep my purse and car keys ready and put them

_____

_ (List place) in order to leave quickly.

C. I can tell_____ and _____ about the violence and request they call the police if they hear suspicious noises coming from my house.

D. I can teach my children how to use the telephone to contact the police and fire department.

E. I will use _____ as my code for my children or my friends so they can call for help.

F. If I have to leave my home, I will go

_____

G. I can also teach some of these strategies to some or all of my Children. When I expect we are going to have an argument, I will try to move to a space that

is lowest risk, such as

_____

(Try to avoid arguments in the bathroom, garage, and kitchen, near weapons or in rooms without access to an outside door).

I will use my judgment and intuition. If the situation is very serious, I can give my partner what he/she wants to calm him/her down. I have to protect myself until we are out of danger.

Step 2: Safety when preparing to leave

Battered women frequently leave the residence they share with the battering partner. Leaving must be done with a careful plan in order to increase safety. Batterers often strike back when they believe that a battered woman is leaving the relationship.

I can use some or all of the following safety strategies:

A. I will leave money and an extra set of keys with

_____ so that I can leave quickly.

B. I will keep copies of important documents or keys at

_____

C. I will open a saving account by _____ to increase my independence.

D. Other things I can do to increase my independence include

_____

_____

_____

E. The domestic violence hotline number in my city is

_____

The National Domestic Violence Hotline number is 1-800-799-SAFE. I can seek shelter by calling this number.

F. I can purchase a pre-paid phone and keep it with me at all times.

I understand that if I use my telephone at home or our family cell phone, the following month the

telephone bill will tell my batterer those numbers I called after I left.

To keep my telephone communications confidential, either I must use my prepaid cell phone or I might get a friend to add me to her cell phone plan for a limited time when I first leave.

G. I will check with
_____ and

_____ to see who would be able to let me stay with them or lend me some money.

H. I can leave extra clothes with

_____

_____

I. I will sit down and review my safety plan every_____ in order to plan the safest way to leave the residence. My friend or domestic violence advocate _____ has agreed to help me review this plan.

J. I will rehearse my escape plan and, as appropriate, practice it with my children.

Step 3: Safety in my own home

There are many things a woman can do to increase her safety in her own residence. It may be impossible to do everything at once, but safety measures can be added step-by-step. Safety measures to use should include:

I can change the locks on my doors and windows as soon as possible. I can replace wooden doors with steel/metal doors.

I can install security systems including additional locks, window bars, poles to wedge against doors, and electronic system, etc.

I can purchase rope ladders to be used for escape from second-story windows.

I can install smoke detectors and protectors and purchase fire extinguishers for each floor in my house or apartment.

I can install an outside lighting system that lights up when a person is coming close to the house.

I will teach my children how to use the telephone to make a collect call to me and to

_____

(friend/minister/other) in the event my partner takes the children.

I will tell people who take care of my children which people have permission to pick up my children and that my partner is not permitted to do so. The people I will inform about pick-up permission
include:_____

School

_____

Daycare

_____

Babysitter

_____

Sunday School Teacher

_____

Teacher

Others

I can inform the following people that my partner no longer resides with me and they should call the police if he is observed near my home.

_____

Neighbors

_____

Pastor

_____

Friends

ABOUT THE AUTHOR

As a native of Chicago, Darlene's life changed forever when her youngest sister Ina Mae was lost to domestic violence. This tragedy prompted her to develop an organization where women in crisis could go to receive help and resources to escape potentially deadly situations.

The Ina Mae Greene Foundation-For My Sisters a 501c3 is an educational, resource and information foundation. The foundation's objective is to raise awareness about the atrocities of domestic abuse. Darlene is a very passionate speaker and lecturer on the topic of domestic violence and domestic abuse.

In addition to conducting dating violence's awareness training and teen dating violence education, Ms. Greene lectures on how to leave an abusive relationship safely. She is the author of two important Domestic Violence safety and resource books;

"WHEN YOU LIVE IN FEAR: HOW TO GET OUT OF A RELATIONSHIP THAT IS KILLING YOU!" This book is a resource and information guide for victims of domestic abuse who are trying to leave a dangerous relationship, and

BLOOD RELATIVES: BREAKING, THE CYCLE... BREAKING THE SILENCE (EXPOSING THE UGLINESS OF DOMESTIC VIOLENCE), the true story of three women in Darlene's family who were murdered by men they dated; and her latest book- **"Big Momma Didn't Tell Me**! Based on the real life account of Curtis's family lineage, this fictional portrayal reveals how the devastating effect of relationship violence rips from a family all that is dear while drawing them closer together in a love rooted in the presence of a matriarchal figure known affectionately as Big Momma.

Darlene lives in Dallas Texas with her husband, son, two steps sons, and six grandchildren.

REFERENCE PAGE

1. New International Version –Holy Bible
2. Quotations.about.com
3. Quote garden.com
4. Brainy Quote

The Ina Mae Greene Foundation For My Sisters is a 501c3 not for profit organization that provides life saving information to victims of domestic abuse. To read more about the work we do in the community to raise awareness about domestic violence please visit our website—
www.inamaegreene.org

BECAUSE THE ROAD TO SAFETY SHOULD NOT BE A DEAD-END!

Copyright 2015 © Darlene Greene

Facebook

Twitter

www.ingramcontent.com/pod-product-compliance
Lightning Source LLC
Chambersburg PA
CBHW051947160426
43198CB00013B/2337